THE BASICS OF
BEAD
STRINGING

By
DAVE CHAMPION

Illustrations and Graphic Production by
Mel Anderson Graphic Design

Copyright © 1985 by Borjay
Third Printing (Revised) July 1986
Published by Borjay
1636 11th Street
Santa Monica, CA 90404
All rights reserved.

Library of Congress Catalog Card Number: 85-71889
ISBN 0-9615353-0-X

CONTENTS

Introduction

Beads are one of the most ancient and diversified forms of personal adornment used by mankind. Every known culture uses or has used beads in one form or another.

To help both the beginner and the professional pursue this time honored art form is the aim of this book.

Dave Champion wrote this book just as if he were personally teaching the reader how to string beads for fun or profit. Dave has lectured and been involved in the lapidary and jewelry arts all his adult life and is most sought after for his knowledge and skills.

In this book you will find most of the information needed to start simple bead stringing projects, and progress right up to doing your own designing.

This book is written to make bead stringing simple. Keep in mind, however, that this is an art form like any other craft. There is more to it than simply lacing beads on a string. There is a right way and a wrong way, and by following the skills shown in this book together with your own creativity you can produce professional quality bead necklaces.

Learning to string beads can be fun! It need not be difficult or expensive unless you choose to make it so.

Dave Champion, author.

1. The Anatomy Of A Bead Necklace

The basic bead necklace is made of several parts as illustrated and described here. These are the most commonly used, with many more types being available, particularly clasps, that serve specific functions in more elaborate and multi-strand designs.

The most popular length of a necklace is 18 to 24 inches. Following is a list of typical names given to specific lengths.

	Approximate Finished Lengths	
Name	Loose	Knotted
Choker	14 inches	16 inches
Princess	16 - 18 inches	18 - 20 inches
Matinee	20 - 24 inches	23 - 27 inches
Opera	32 - 34 inches	35 - 37 inches
Bracelets	6 - 7 inches	7 - 8 inches

Beads, of course, come in a huge variety of materials, shapes, and sizes. Gemstone varieties are typically round but may also be found in other shapes, i.e. tube, square, diamond shape, etc. Chips or nuggets of gemstone materials may also be used. These are polished by a tumbling method and make interesting and beautiful necklace designs.

Rondells, or spacers, are used between beads as enhancers to the design or, as the name suggests, spacers to fill areas and endings where the quantity of the main beads is limited in numbers sufficient to construct the desired finished length. Names and shapes of rondells are given below.

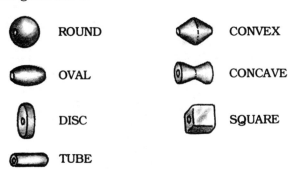

ROUND   CONVEX

OVAL   CONCAVE

DISC   SQUARE

TUBE

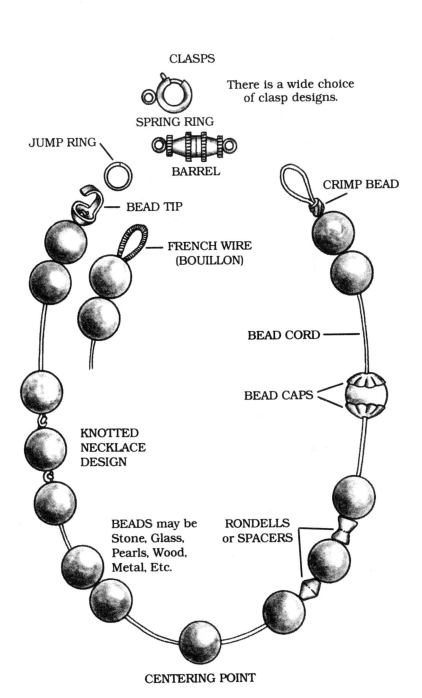

CLASPS

There is a wide choice
of clasp designs.

SPRING RING

JUMP RING

BARREL

BEAD TIP

FRENCH WIRE
(BOUILLON)

CRIMP BEAD

BEAD CORD

BEAD CAPS

KNOTTED
NECKLACE
DESIGN

BEADS may be
Stone, Glass,
Pearls, Wood,
Metal, Etc.

RONDELLS
or SPACERS

CENTERING POINT

7

2. Selecting The Tools

As with any art form or craft, the selection and use of the right tools and supplies is essential for success. And, bead stringing is no exception. Proper tools will allow you to achieve professional results with ease and enjoyment.

Bead Boards

There are several types of bead boards available to the stringer. The typical board is a hardwood plank with several grooves cut into the surface. The grooves keep the beads from rolling away as you maneuver them into a desired design and then keep them in the proper position for stringing.

The style of board is largely a matter of personal preference. Traditional hardwood boards come with natural finish or velvet coverings. The newer molded plastic trays have curved grooves and storage compartments. Some boards have measurement scales on them. Cost will range from $5.00 to $20.00 each.

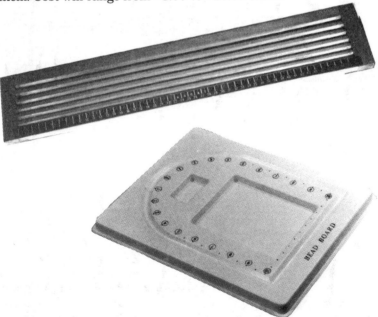

A traditional hardwood bead board containing six grooves with measuring scale is shown here with a natural finish, but may also be found with velvet covering. The molded plastic bead tray features a curved groove and storage compartments with a measuring scale printed on the surface.

Tweezers

Three types of tweezers should be found in the collection of tools for bead stringers. The bead knotting tweezer has extra sharp points and a slender shank which makes it invaluable for tying knots and pulling needles through bead holes. They measure about 4 or 5 inches, are made of stainless steel and cost about $5.00.

Stone holding tweezers are longer tweezers with fairly sharp points and narrow shanks. Tips are usually serrated on the inside for gripping action. You will find these very useful for picking up small beads, grading and separating. They are about 6½ inches long and cost about $5.00.

Teflon coated tweezers are used for handling pearls and other soft materials that might otherwise be damaged in handling. A generous portion of the tips are coated for protection from scratching and abrasion. The tips are cup shaped to provide a positive but safe grip on the bead or pearl. Cost is about $10.00.

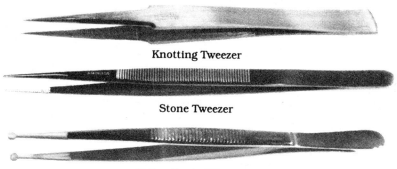

Knotting Tweezer

Stone Tweezer

Teflon Coated Tweezer

Needles and Awls

You will also need one or more sewing needles. (These are not what you will be using to string beads however, we will discuss bead stringing needles later in this book.) Sewing needles are great for seating knots in bead tips, knotting between small pearls, etc. Also used in cleaning drill holes in beads, as well as picking out cement and impacted knots when restringing. For better control of the needle, you may wish to set the needle in a wooden dowel handle or use it in a pin vise.

A commercially manufactured awl is also available, serving the same function as the sewing needle. They are made of stainless steel and have a sturdy shank which will undoubtedly serve the bead stringer with a lifetime of service.

Adhesives

You will want a fast-drying type of cement, such as used by jewelers. Ending knots should have a drop of cement applied. This helps to keep the knots from unraveling. White glue, clear nail polish, or craft cement works well. A drop of adhesive on the jump rings helps to keep the ring from pulling open. Instant cements, such as cyanoacrylates, are not recommended as they tend to flow along the cord cementing several beads together into a solid, stiff, strand.

Bond 527 is a good choice for cementing requirements in bead stringing. 'Super' or 'Instant' type adhesives are not recommended.

Pliers

Two types of pliers are required for professional results in bead stringing. Round nose pliers with long and smooth jaws are used for closing bead tips, curving wire such as jump rings and looping ends of eye pins, etc. They are generally 5½ inches long and cost about $10.00.

Chain nose pliers have a wide variety of uses. In bead stringing, they are a must for locking crimp beads, attaching needles to bead cord and to straighten or open jump rings, etc. They are also a handy holding instrument when forming wire. I recommend a long nose, smooth jaw plier about 5 inches in length. Cost is about $10.00.

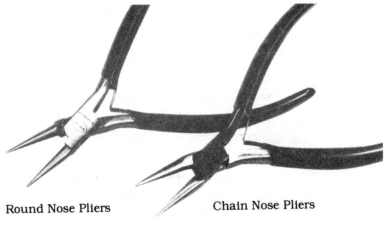

Round Nose Pliers   Chain Nose Pliers

Rulers and Gauges

A yard stick or a 24" ruler marked in inches and millimeters is the handiest device for laying out your beads accurately.

To maintain accurate uniform sizes on tapered strands with proper balance a pocket gauge is a must. This is an inexpensive instrument that measures in inches and millimeters.

A flexible tape should also be included in your tool collection for measuring cord lengths needed for various projects.

Pocket Gauge

Scissors

A good quality, medium size scissors with very sharp cutting edges is a must for cutting cord. I prefer scissors with longer handles and shorter cutting blades as they often offer much sharper cuts. It is extremely important that you keep the blades sharp. Dull blades have a tendency to cause the thread to unravel when it is cut, which will lead to all kinds of problems.

Scissors with long handles and short cutting blades are preferred.

Eyeglasses and Magnifiers

A precision Optivisor or Opticaid magnifier permits unrestricted use of both hands and helps reduce eye strain while working on small beads and intricate designs.

Magnifiers are available for 4", 6", 8", 10" and 14" focal lengths. Focal length is the distance between the workpiece and the magnifier when the magnifier is in focus. Choose the most comfortable distance for you.

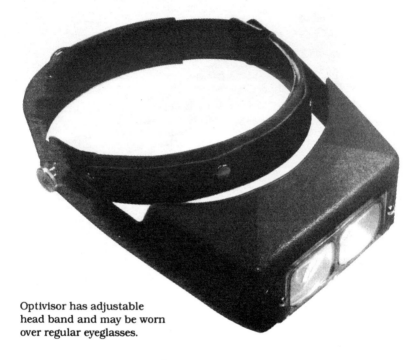

Optivisor has adjustable head band and may be worn over regular eyeglasses.

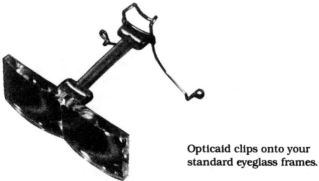

Opticaid clips onto your standard eyeglass frames.

Sources of Supply for Tools

Look under 'Jeweler's Supplies and Findings' or 'Lapidary Shops' in the yellow pages of your local telephone directory. Lapidary trade or hobby magazines should contain advertisements and listings of a selection of suppliers.

Tool Checklist

Do you have all the tools you will need to start your bead stringing projects?

_____ Bead Board
_____ Knotting Tweezers
_____ Stone Holding Tweezers
_____ Teflon Coated Tweezers (optional)
_____ Sewing Needles or Awl
_____ Bond 527 Cement (or similar cement)
_____ Round Nose Pliers
_____ Chain Nose Pliers
_____ Yardstick or Long Ruler
_____ Pocket Gauge
_____ Flexible Measuring Tape
_____ Scissors
_____ Magnifier (optional)

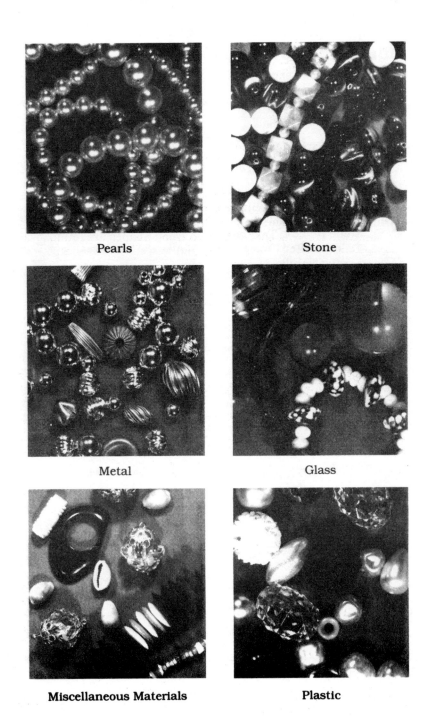

Pearls

Stone

Metal

Glass

Miscellaneous Materials

Plastic

14

3. Selecting Beads

Beads are available in an almost endless variety of types, shapes, sizes and colors. For brevity, I have listed the general divisions into which most beads and bead-types may conveniently be fitted. Several materials, although diverse in nature, are grouped together in one type catagory, as their treatment in beading is virtually identical.

Pearls

Whether natural or cultured, pearls are handled alike in the stringing process. Colors may be white, cream, yellow, blue, pink, grey or black with varying shades in each color. Shapes are round, oval, baroque, Biwa (rice or freshwater), and Mabe. The latter are rarely strung as beads.

Stone

This division covers all materials from soft soapstone to semi-precious gem materials of medium hardness, and continues right up to diamonds and other hard precious gems. Most opaque gem or stone beads are cut round, oval, square, tubular, etc. − while most translucent and transparent gems are faceted. The shapes, colors and patterns found in natural stones are endless, providing the designer with unlimited creative possibilities.

Metal

Metal beads include both solid (cast) and hollow (formed) varieties. Shapes are limitless, but usually round, oval, fluted or tubular. Metal beads are available in a variety of materials including karat gold, gold filled, silver and non-precious alloys. The non-precious metal beads are usually Rhodium (silver color) or Hamilton (gold color) plated. Metal beads are most commonly used as spacers, enhancements or accents, but may also be used exclusively in a design.

Glass

Glass beads date back over 4,000 years and are available in every color of the rainbow. Sizes range from a tiny 1mm to large marble sizes. Glass beads may be found in every conceivable shape imaginable. They might be multi-colored, opaque or transparent, or even combined with metal strips or flakes.

Ceramic

The history and description of ceramic beads reads very similar to glass varieties. In addition to their unlimited variety of color and design, they are sometimes made as 'effigy' beads, as the Scarab beads so popular a few years ago.

Plastic

Probably the most prolific source of beads currently being manufactured is from the plastics industry. Plastic beads are not only inexpensive, but are available in every conceivable size, shape and color. Plastics can simulate stones, ceramics, wood, glass and metal, as well as offer some characteristics unique to themselves.

Miscellaneous Materials

This group of beads include rare and more common materials, such as amber, wood, seeds, shells, 'mother-of-pearl', etc. A wide range of sizes, colors and shapes are available. Of particular interest are antique and ethnic beads that depict an era or people across the country or around the world.

Selecting your beads can be a fun and exciting experience. Your imagination and personal taste should dictate selection. If you have a definite idea in mind, select those beads that will fill your need. If you like to play with colors and shapes, acquire a variety of beads with which to design. Until you become familiar with the basic techniques of bead stringing however, I do suggest that you begin with medium size beads of uniform size. Plastic, stone or glass beads are ideal materials for beginning projects.

How Many Beads Do You Need?

The chart below will enable you to determine just how many beads you will need to complete a strand of beads of uniform size at various lengths.

		Length of Strand	
Bead Size	16"	18"	24"
4mm	100	112	153
6mm	68	76	100
8mm	50	56	76
10mm	40	45	61

Beads are usually measured in millimeters (mm). Here is a visual conversion scale that will help you to start thinking and seeing 'metric'.

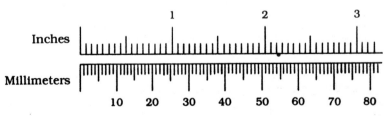

The varieties and combinations of beads are endless.

4. Selecting Bead Stringing Materials

Bead Cord

There are many types of cord or thread available for the bead stringer. Each is selected for the particular size, color, strength or effect it will have on the finished product.

The most commonly used cords are: Silk, Nylon, Tigertail, and Monofilament.

Selecting the right bead cord for your project requires two important considerations:

1) The thread must be able to go through the smallest hole of the beads you are stringing.

2) The bead stringing cord must be able to support the weight of your necklace, bracelet, etc. Use the largest cord, or multiples thereof, that will pass through the smallest hole of your beads without fraying.

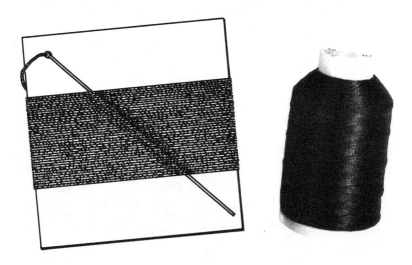

Silk and nylon bead cord are available on individual cards with a bead stringing needle attached, or on bulk spools.

Silk and Nylon

Silk and nylon bead cord are manufactured with a very tight triple twist that provide the materials with surprising strength and durability. We are discussing them together as they are very similar in working characteristics, and for the most part, it is a matter of personal preference as to which is better.

Here are some points to consider when making your selection between silk and nylon cord:

1) Nylon and silk both stretch over a period of time, but silk tends to stretch less.
2) Nylon bead cord is more resistant to fraying than silk bead cord.
3) Silk is better to use when you're tying knots between pearls and other types of beads because it is slicker and makes better and easier knots.
4) By tradition, silk is always used when stringing pearls.
5) Nylon, by its chemical nature, is more resistant to rot and decay than silk.
6) Nylon, size for size, tends to be slightly stronger than silk.
7) Both are available in a variety of colors. However, there is a wider choice with nylon which may also be easier to find.

This is a partial list of colors that are available, with recommendations for using each with natural stones:

Color	Stone
White	Pearls, Rock Crystal
Pink	Coral
Dark Pink	Rose Quartz, Coral
Red	Ruby, Coral
Maroon	Garnet
Yellow	Light Amber, Tigereye
Rust	Amber, Carnelian
Dark Blue	Lapis Lazuli
Lilac	Amethyst (light)
Violet	Amethyst (dark)
Aqua	Turquoise, Aquamarine
Bright Green	Peridot, Malachite
Light Green	Jade
Beige	Pearls, Amber, Carnelian
Brown	Tigereye
Grey	Grey Pearls, Hematite
Black	Onyx, Black Pearls, Obsidian

If you are stringing plastic, glass, ceramic or wood beads, select complimentary colors of bead cord to the beads you are using. Multicolor strands of beads are typically strung on white or black cord.

Synopsis of Silk and Nylon Bead Cord

Available: Jewelry tool supply houses.

Color: Variety of many colors.

Strength: Average

Sizes: All colors of nylon and silk are available in the following sizes:

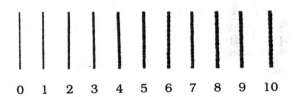

Packaged: Spools and on cards. Cards come with 6.5 feet of thread with bead needle attached. Spools vary in lengths depending on the size of cord.

Advantages: Flexibility of finished product, beads hang well and natural. Knots hold well. Many colors available.

Disadvantages: Possibility of fraying. Not strong enough for very heavy beads and necklaces. May stretch over period of time.

Tigertail

Tigertail is simply a name given to a strong bead stringing material that is made of fine twisted wires coated with plastic. It is a miniature coated cable.

Beads which are metal, large or heavy and have sharp edges, will require a stronger, more durable bead stringing cord. Tigertail is ideal as it will support the weight of heavy or large beads and will allow the finished necklace to hang correctly when worn. Hollow metal beads or stone beads with sharp edges, while lighter in weight, virtually require stringing on tigertail, as they will soon cut non-metallic cords in two.

This is a spool of plastic coated fine steel cable called Tigertail. It is readily found in jewelry tool supply houses.

Synopsis of Tigertail

Available: Jewelry tool supply houses.

Color: Silver or brass.

Strength: Strong. Ideal for large Indian style necklaces.

Sizes: Available in 3 sizes: .012" (thin), .015" (medium), .020" (heavy).

Packaged: 30, 100, and 1,000 foot spools.

Advantages: Strength. Inexpensive. Needs no needle.

Disadvantages: Not as flexible as other bead cords. Does not hang well if used with lightweight beads. Has a tendency to kink. Usually requires the use of crimp beads as knots do not hold well.

Monofilament

Monofilament is nylon fishing line that doubles as a general purpose, inexpensive bead cord. It is a clear material that is stiff enough to use without a needle, and strong enough that a single strand is sufficient. It is generally used for inexpensive or costume beads.

Synopsis of Monofilament

Available: Sporting goods stores.

Color: Transparent blue, green, yellow or clear.

Strength: Strong. A variety of breaking tests available. 6 lb. to 40 lb. test is the usual range for bead stringing.

Packaged: Small and large spools of varying lengths to 1000 yards.

Advantages: Inexpensive. Good for heavy beads.

Disadvantages: Too heavy a line will give necklace a rigid or stiff look, and will retain coiled nature from spool that is difficult to straighten. Special knotting techniques may be required to prevent slippage or untying.

Monofilament fishing line is available from sporting goods stores in a variety of breaking tests, colors and lengths.

Needles

Needles designed for bead stringing are recommended for use with silk or nylon cords. They make the job easier and result in a more professional product by preventing cord from unraveling or fraying at the ends.

Flexible twisted wire needles are available in three sizes:

Fine
Medium
Heavy

They have large eyes which will close when pulled through the first bead. They are sold in packages of one dozen and one gross. Cost is approximately $2.00 per dozen or $12.00 per gross.

Silk and nylon bead cords come with a twisted wire needle attached when purchased in 6.5 foot lengths on cards. The needle is usually discarded after use.

A solid steel type needle similar to one used for sewing, but very fine, can also be used.

Findings

The availablility of findings (components) that can be used in your necklace design can and does fill many pages of catalogs. We will attempt to review only some of the more basic types. "Findings" is a term used in the jewelry industry to describe manufactured silver, gold and base metal items, such as clasps, jump rings, spring rings, etc., which are used in the make-up of finished jewelry items.

Clasps are the connectors you find on bracelets that cannot be slipped over the hand, or necklaces that will not easily go over the head in order to be worn. They allow you to disconnect and re-connect the ends of strands for wearing. Clasps may be simple or fancy in design and come in a variety of sizes. Some offer more security than others, making accidental disconnection nearly impossible. Care should be taken in choosing a clasp appropriate to the size of the beads used. Too large a clasp on a strand of small beads will appear clumsy and out of place. Too small a clasp on a strand of large beads may not hold the weight and could readily break. Clasps are available in base metals, plated, gold filled, sterling silver, and karat gold.

Jump rings are used to connect the clasp to the ends of the bead strand. Jump rings are either round or oval in shape, and are simply a metal ring or wire with a slit that allows the ring to be opened for connecting to clasp and cord. They, too, are available in base metals, plated, gold filled, sterling silver, and karat gold. Your more expensive pieces should utilize gold filled, sterling silver or karat gold jump rings, particularly if you intend to solder the slit for security.

Another type of jump ring is actually called a split ring. Split rings are very small double circles of wire that are similar in design to a key ring. While they do offer more security than the standard jump ring, they are somewhat more difficult to attach.

Bead tips are used to conceal the final knots, or endings of the cord, and are then connected to the jump ring or clasp. The use of bead tips add that professional touch to bead stringing. They are available in base metal, nickel silver, gold filled, sterling silver and karat gold in varying sizes.

Crimp beads are tiny brass or silver plated brass beads that are used at the cord ends rather than tying knots. Since tigertail and monofilament are difficult to tie, the crimp bead is used to clamp the cord together forming a small loop on the end. Crimps should not be used with twisted nylon or silk as they will likely cut through the cord.

Bead caps are plain, fluted or decorated small concave discs used to set-off individual beads. They are used on both sides of selected, larger beads as decorations or to highlight areas in the necklace. Caps are made of base metals, plated, gold filled, sterling silver and karat gold in varying sizes. Solid simplicity or fancy filigree patterns are available.

French wire (bouillon) is a hollow, spring-like coil of fine silver wire that has been copper plated and dipped in gold. Old timers prefer using French wire as a connector between the strand and the clasp. Bouillon replaces the jump ring and reinforces this connection between the clasp and the strand. It is available in fine, medium and heavy weight and is usually sold by the inch. It is not very expensive, especially since only about one-half inch is usually used in each ending.

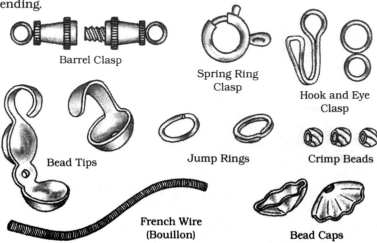

Barrel Clasp

Spring Ring Clasp

Hook and Eye Clasp

Bead Tips

Jump Rings

Crimp Beads

French Wire (Bouillon)

Bead Caps

Some of the basic bead necklace findings are shown here. Become familiar with their names and uses.

5. Let's Get Started — First Project

In order to complete this first project, you will need: a beadboard, a selection of beads, bead tips, bead cord with needle, jump rings, clasp, cement, scissors, chain nose pliers, and a medium to large sewing needle.

Gather your beads, supplies and tools together and select a solid flat work surface with ample room to spread your materials out. Working on a TV tray, or holding the bead board in your lap will likely prove to be a poor alternative to a good work bench or table.

If you're not sure as to what beads, findings and cord to choose, we suggest you begin with the following:

1) A 16" loose strung strand of gemstone beads. Select the material that appeals to you and is within your price range. A strand of 6mm beads start from under $5.00 per strand. Loose strung beads will usually come on monofilament line, loosely tied with no findings.

2) A size 3 carded nylon bead cord with needle attached.

3) Size 2½mm wide, gold or silver color bead tips.

4) Gold or silver color barrel clasp.

5) Size 4mm jump rings.

Begin by laying out your design on the bead board. Beads should be kept in the proper design order on the board so they are ready to string in the desired sequence. Use as many beads as necessary to give the desired length to the finished strand, keeping in mind to

Choose a solid flat work surface to rest your bead board on. Using the grooves to retain the beads, layout your design on the bead board and get ready to string.

This exquisite necklace designed by Da-Ru Treasures features 11 - 7½mm by 17mm hand painted porcelain beads, 22 - 6mm rhodonite beads, 30 - 10mm carved aventurine beads strung on pink bead cord with partial knotting. The ends are attached to a vermiel clasp with french wire (bouillon) loops. Total length is 27 inches.

A

A lovely blend of 32 - 7mm by 11mm natural pink pearls and 33 - 4mm amethyst beads are strung on white bead cord in a knotted design by Da-Ru Treasures. Endings have been tied directly to the eyes of the 14K yellow gold bead clasp. Total length is 22 inches.

B

These earring, bracelet, and necklace ensembles were created by Christina's Designs. The set on the top uses 2 gold filled box clasps, a pair of gold filled earposts with 5mm ball and drop, 2 gold filled heading pins, 4 gold filled bead tips, 12 - 3mm by 8mm freshwater rice pearls, 88 - 6mm black onyx beads, 4 - 2mm gold filled beads, and 20 - 3mm gold filled beads. The set on the bottom uses 2 gold filled box clasps, a pair of gold filled earposts with 5mm ball and drop, 4 gold filled heading pins, 4 gold filled bead tips, 68 - 3mm by 8mm freshwater rice pearls, 12 - 6mm Austrian crystal beads, 20 - 4mm Austrian crystal beads, 4 - 2mm gold filled beads, and 19 - 3mm gold filled beads. Each necklace is 18 inches long and the bracelets are 7½ inches long.

C

The faceted bead necklace (left) designed by Dave Champion is 20 inches long and contains 85 - 5mm gemstone beads; 35 amethyst, 20 quartz, 10 citrine, 10 peridot, and 10 aquamarine. 18 - 5mm 14K yellow gold beads have also been incorporated into the design and the ends have been secured with bead tips. The clasp is a 14K yellow gold cylinder style. The large bead necklace (right) from Necklines Design, features 5 - 12mm carved cape amethyst beads, 20 clear quartz crystal rondelles, and 24 - 12mm chalcedony beads. This is a knotted necklace measuring 18 inches and secured at the ends with bead tips. A 14K yellow gold Easy-Loc clasp has been used.

D

Bryn Inohara designed this 21 inch necklace (top) of 70 - 6mm pink coral beads, 6 - 7mm freshwater pearls, and 19 - 3mm 14K yellow gold beads. The ends were fitted with bead tips which secure the 6mm 14k yellow gold ball clasp. The stunning design by Anthony Chavez (bottom) features 20 - 5mm rondelles, 2 - 5mm round, 2 - 6mm round, and 2 - 7mm round sterling silver beads contrasting the 40 - 6mm heart, 42 - 4mm round, and 1 - 8mm round hematite beads. Ends are finished with bead tips and the clasp is a sterling silver fishhook . Total length is 18 inches.

E

The 22 inch necklace by Christina's Designs (inside) was created using 41 -
8mm and 6 - 6mm Mother-of-Pearl beads, 4 - 8mm and 8 - 5½mm by 11mm
hematite beads, and 12 - 3mm gold filled beads. Gold filled fishhook clasp is
secured by the bead tip endings. The 34 inch necklace (outside) is an endless,
knotted design using 82 - 8mm black onyx beads, 12 - 4mm black onyx beads,
6 - 8mm ivory beads, and 1 ivory carving.

F

The endless 32 inch strand (left) contains 30 - 8mm ivory beads, 62 - 8mm dark amethyst beads, 6 - 7mm 14K yellow gold round beads, and 6 - 14K yellow gold rondelles. The purple bead cord has been knotted between the amethyst beads only. Bryn Inohara used 65 - 6mm amethyst beads, 10 - 10mm carved amethyst flowers, and 25 - 3½mm sterling silver rondelles to create this lovely necklace (right). This knotted design using purple bead cord is finished with bead tips and fitted with a sterling silver fishhook clasp. Total length is 23 inches.

G

Christina's Designs provided a striking creation of 90 - 4mm lapis beads, 8 - 3½mm by 7mm freshwater rice pearls, and 16 - 3mm 14K yellow gold beads (top). Ends are secured with bead tips and a 14K yellow gold fishhook clasp was used. Total length is 18 inches. The graduated necklace (bottom) contains 78 - 4mm ivory beads, 30 - 5mm malachite beads, 30 - 6mm malachite beads, and 18 - 8mm malachite beads and measures 29 inches long. The ends have been tied directly to a sterling silver fishhook clasp.

H

calculate the length of the clasp into the total length of your necklace. Don't hesitate to play with your ideas. Move the beads around, changing colors and sizes if you wish, until you're happy with the layout. When you are satisfied with your design, select the largest bead cord that will fit through the beads you have used.

If you are using cord from a spool, cut a length several inches longer than your finished necklace will be, and attach a twisted wire needle to one end. If you are using a ready-to-use cord, remove the cord completely from the card. Stretch cord to its entire length and pull taut to remove any kinks.

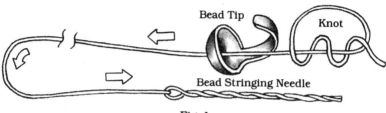

Fig. 1

Now take a bead tip and thread onto cord as shown (Fig. 1). Tie a double overhand knot on the end of the cord and pull it tightly into bead tip cup. Apply cement to knot (Fig. 2) and allow to dry before clipping excess thread off. You may find it easier to apply a drop of cement to the end of a toothpick and in turn apply the cement to the knot in the bead tip. This offers a little more control as you do not want too much cement.

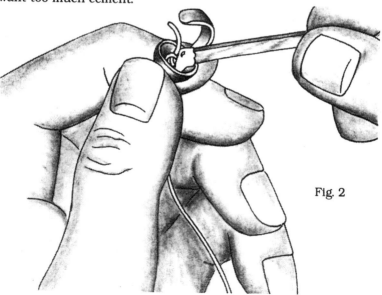

Fig. 2

Fig. 3

You are now ready to begin stringing beads. Simply thread needle through each bead until you have your entire design strung on the cord.

Now attach final bead tip to end as shown (Fig. 3), and tie another double overhand knot. The sewing needle may be used here to aid in working the final knot in as close as possible to the inside of the bead tip cup (Fig. 4).

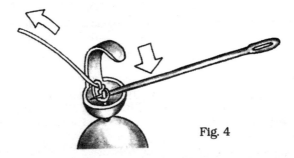

Fig. 4

Be sure the knot is fully concealed and firm against the bead tip before applying a final drop of cement.

If you are going to use jump rings between the bead tips and the clasp, close the hook on the bead tip now by gripping the end of the hook with chain nose pliers and rolling closed (Fig. 5).

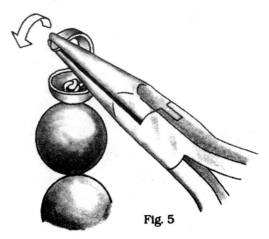

Fig. 5

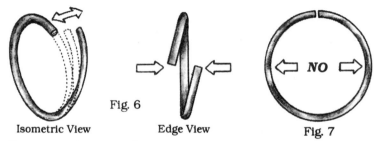

Fig. 6

Isometric View   Edge View   Fig. 7

Now open a jump ring by twisting apart at slit. Apply side pressure as shown (Fig. 6) to open and close jump rings. Do not try to pry apart by enlarging the diameter of the ring. It will surely weaken and likely break, and will not close completely (Fig. 7). Attach bead tip and eye of clasp to jump ring and close it in the same fashion as you opened it. Apply a small drop of cement onto the joint of the jump ring to strengthen. Repeat for other end of strand.

You may elect to eliminate the jump rings from your necklace by simply attaching the bead tip directly to the clasp. Some clasps, however, require a jump ring for mobility. The clasp should move freely on the end for ease of fastening.

Congratulations on the completion of your first hand made bead necklace! You have now learned the basic steps in assembling this popular jewelry item. But, don't stop here, there's more on the way!

If you have followed directions correctly, you will have a beautiful finished necklace similar to this one.

6. The Hand Knotted Necklace

A knotted necklace is a design in which the bead cord is knotted between each bead on the strand. The secret to knotting is easily learned and mastered with a little practice. Silk or nylon bead cord can be used in knotted designs while other cord materials are either too stiff or do not hold tight knots easily. Pearls and most types of gemstone strands are most attractive when knotted.

Reasons for knotting are:

1) Design. Each bead is shown to its best advantage.

2) Safety. Should the strand break, only one pearl or bead is dropped.

3) Protection. The beads are protected from rubbing against one another. Metals, softer gemstones, and especially pearls, should have this protection.

Some points to remember for good hand knotting results:

1) Try to make each knot the same size, shape and distance from the bead.

2) Try not to twist the cord in various directions.

3) Maintain a tension that will prevent the beads from drawing up, appearing stiff, or hanging too loose and appearing disconnected.

4) Knotting adds 1 to 2 inches, or more, to the length of a strand of beads, depending on the size of the cord used, and the number of beads in the strand.

Single Strand (Single Cord Method)

To begin stringing a knotted strand of pearls or gemstones, choose the largest size thread that will fit through the holes in the beads. This thread needs to be at least twice the length of the finished strand. This project uses only a single strand of bead cord, with a single knot between each bead.

Start with a single strand of bead cord and attach a bead tip with a knot pulled tightly into the bead tip cup. Apply some cement to the knot and allow it to dry before clipping any excess thread. Refer back to the first project if you need to refresh your memory about setting on the bead tip.

Now thread all pearls or beads onto the strand. Yes, even though we're going to be knotting between each bead, this technique requires that all the beads go on the cord first. After all the beads or pearls are on the thread, tie a slip knot between the needle and beads, close to the needle (Fig. 8). This will keep the beads from sliding off the cord.

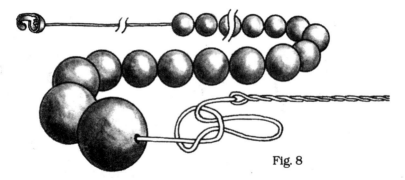

Fig. 8

Push the beads as far down toward the needle as possible until they are held by the slip knot.

Now make another knot (single overhand) on the cord just behind the bead tip. Using your tweezer (Fig. 9-A) or sewing needle (Fig. 9-B), draw the knot in close to the bead tip as shown. Pay attention to the illustrations — the needle or tweezer enters the knot parallel to the cord coming from the finished end, following the same path as the cord. Entering the loop over the cross-over will put the loop between the needle and the cord and cause the knot to flip when you try to slide it. This could lead to the knot being cinched up too quickly and not seated properly against the tip. Now, keeping the knot against the bead tip, pull on the cord to tighten the knot and withdraw the needle or tweezer.

Fig. 9-A   Fig. 9-B

A little knot tying practice with another cord will help you learn how to draw the knot in tightly against the tip and, later on, each bead. Using the knotting tweezer is easier, since the knot actually slides down the tweezer rather than on the cord itself. Grip the cord with the tweezer tips as close as possible to the bead tip or bead and pull the cord at a right angle to the tweezer as it slides down the tips. Cinch the knot tight when it slips off the end of the tweezer. As it simply cannot go anywhere other than off the end of the tweezer, premature tightening is nearly impossible.

After you have properly knotted the tip, slide up your first bead to the knot just made. Loop the thread around your first and second

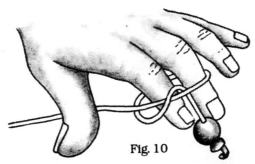

Fig. 10

fingers, holding the loop open in order to drop the already finished end of your strand through this loop (Fig. 10). Slide your tweezer (Fig. 11-A) or needle (Fig. 11-B) into this knot in the direction shown (parallel to the cord coming out of the bead), and pull the knot tight against the first bead as you did with the bead tip.

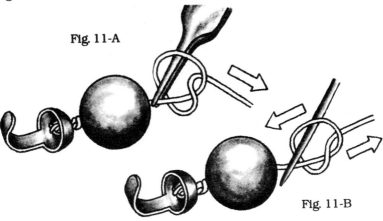

Fig. 11-A

Fig. 11-B

Slide the next bead up and repeat the procedure. Continue sliding up new beads and tying knots until necklace is completely knotted with a final knot retaining the last bead.

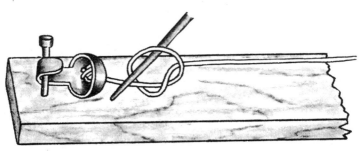

Fig. 12

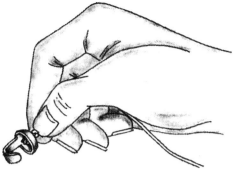

Fig. 13

Hints: You may find it easier to anchor the finished end using a board with a small nail hamered into the center of the top about an inch from the end. Hooking the bead tip on the nail keeps the end from wandering, which may help you in sliding knots with a needle (Fig. 12). When a knot is released from a needle or tweezer, use your thumbnail to push the knot tight (Fig. 13).

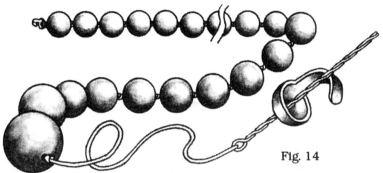

Fig. 14

After retaining the last bead on the strand, untie the slip knot near the needle and thread your final bead tip onto the cord inserting the needle through the bottom of the tip (Fig. 14). But, don't tie it off yet — we're going to show you a new way to do it.

Cut the thread off about 3 inches from the end of the beads. Split or unravel the twisted thread into two strands, separating down to the

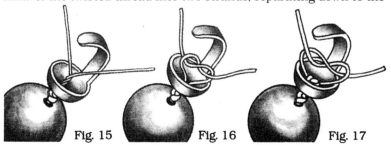

Fig. 15   Fig. 16   Fig. 17

Fig. 18

bead tip. Tie a square knot with these two strands, pulling each half of the knot tightly into the cup of the bead tip. That's the first half tied (Fig. 16) and pulled tightly into the bead tip, then the second half (Fig. 17) on top of the first and pulled tightly. A square knot is made by crossing over each half in opposite directions. Crossing the same way on each half of the knot produces a 'Granny' knot which is apt to untie. Seal the knot with cement and allow to dry before trimming off excess thread.

Your necklace is complete, and all that remains is to attach the clasp of your choice to the bead tips (Fig. 18) and it is ready to wear. Close the hooks on the bead tips with fine-tipped chain nose pliers or round nose pliers. If you choose to use jump rings between ends and clasp, refer to first project instructions.

Single Strand (Doubled Cord Method)

Now that you have mastered the single cord method, we will show you another technique in knotting necklaces using bulk cord from a spool.

Select a bead cord of a size that when doubled will fit comfortably through the bead hole, but not too loosely or your knots will pass through the beads.

You will need a length of bead cord from the spool approximately six times longer than the length of the finished strand.

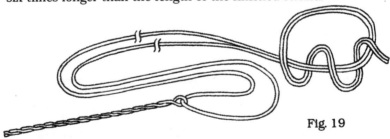

Fig. 19

Thread the bead cord through the eye of the needle and pull the cord until the ends are even. Tie the ends together with a double overhand knot (Fig. 19) to prevent the beads from slipping off. Pull this knot into a bead tip and tie a second knot firmly against the base of the bead tip. Proceed with your stringing and knotting per previous instructions.

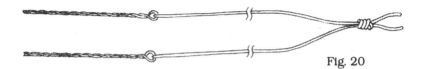

Fig. 20

Single Strand (Two Cord Method)

We use two individual bead cords in this method, joining them at the far end (from the needle) with a double overhand knot (Fig. 20), threading both cords through the bead tip and pulling the knot firmly into the cup of the bead tip. Using this method, a square knot is tied after each bead is strung. DO NOT string all the beads first, as in the previous instructions. Use a slightly smaller diameter bead cord than the doubled cord method, in order to easily slip both cords through the bead holes.

Fig. 21-A   Fig. 21-B

After the bead tip is strung, tie a square knot firmly against the tip (Fig. 21-A and 21-B). Now string the first bead onto the double cord, threading each needle through the bead one at a time. Push the bead as tightly against the bead tip as possible.

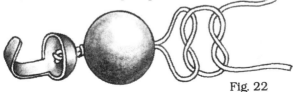

Fig. 22

Next, tie a square knot tightly against the first bead (Fig. 22). Thread a second bead onto each of the two cords (one at a time). Tie a square knot against the second bead and thread on the third bead.

Continue tying square knots and adding beads until the strand of beads is completed. You will find this method especially useful when stringing large beads, such as wood, amber, crystal, etc., or beads with very large holes.

At the end, the final bead tip is added in the same fashion as individual beads, except that it is not necessary to split the individual bead cords. Just use the two cords to tie a final square knot.

After you have sealed both end knots with cement, allowed them to dry, clipped off all excess cord and attached your clasp, you have finished another project.

7. Alternate Endings

Continuous Strand

Any necklace with a finished length of 24" or more can be made into a continuous strand, i.e., a complete circle of beads without a clasp. This is accomplished with the following method: a slip knot is used to start the stringing. No bead tip or clasp is used. Knotting starts between the third and fourth beads, with NO knots between the first and second, or the second and third beads (Fig. 23).

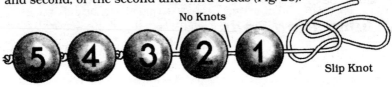

Fig. 23

After completing the stringing and knotting, no knot is tied after the last bead. The bead cord is next run through the first bead (Fig. 24) (two cords are now through this bead), and a knot is securely tied around the starting cord between the first and second bead (Fig. 25-A). Be sure the necklace is first pulled tightly so that no space is left at the end.

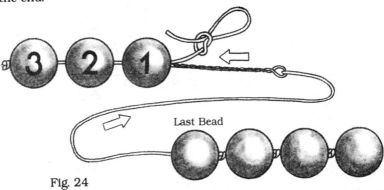

Fig. 24

When this knot is secure (between the first and second bead), run the corded needle through the second bead. After pulling the cord tight, tie a knot around the starting cord between the second and third bead (Fig. 25-B).

Untie the slip knot from the starting end of the bead cord, and tie a knot securely around finishing end of the bead cord between the last bead and the first bead (Fig. 25-C). Seal all three of the last knots tied with cement, allow it to dry completely and trim off the remaining ends. Your continuous strand necklace is complete. NOTE: For

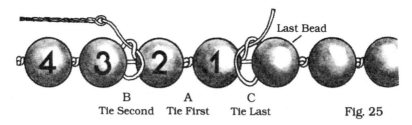

B   A   C

Tie Second   Tie First   Tie Last   Fig. 25

clarity, some space is shown between bead #1 and last bead in the illustration. In practice, there should be no space here. These beads should be tight against one another.

Jump Ring Ends

On occasion, it may be desirable to complete a necklace without attaching a clasp. When this occurs, a jump ring ending is the simplest solution. Usually, it is better — and safer — if the jump ring is soldered. This will prevent a break in the ring through which the bead cord could slip off.

As with the continuous strand, start with a slip knot to keep the beads on the cord. Run the cord through the second and first beads (in that order) without knotting in between. Wrap the cord twice through the jump ring (Fig. 26), and reinsert the needle into the first bead in the opposite direction of the initial threading. Pull tightly and tie a knot around the starting cord between the first and second bead.

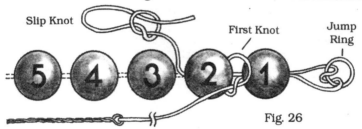

Fig. 26

Insert the needle and pull the cord through the second bead, then string the third, fourth and fifth beads. Untie the starting slip knot and tie this end securely around the cord between the second and third beads (Fig. 27). Seal both of these starting knots with cement before continuing with the stringing and knotting of the entire necklace.

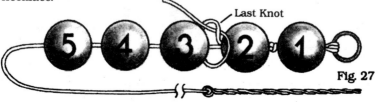

Fig. 27

Repeat this same starting procedure with the next-to-last and the last bead on the other end of your necklace. Do not tie knots between the last three beads on the finishing end of the necklace. Instead, run the bead cord through these last three beads after knotting between the third and fourth beads from the end.

Wrap cord twice through a second jump ring, then reinsert the needle and pull the cord back through the last bead. This is done in the opposite direction of the cord already coming through. Pull cord tight and tie a knot around the cord between the last and next-to-last bead. Insert the needle and pull the cord through the next-to-last bead. Tie it securely around the cord between next-to-last and third-to-last beads (Fig. 28).

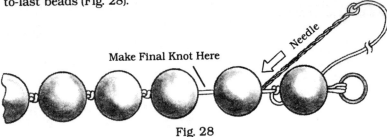

Make Final Knot Here

Needle

Fig. 28

Seal both of these knots with cement, allow to dry, trim off remaining ends and the necklace is complete.

This same method may be used, of course, when tying directly onto the loops of a clasp, when the use of an intermediate jump ring is not indicated. However, when using continuous jump rings at each end of a necklace, any available clasp may be attached, or a defective clasp may be replaced, without restringing the beads, providing that the color of jump ring matches the color of the clasp used.

French Wire (Bouillon)

Bouillon is a tiny "spring" of silver wire, or gold plated silver wire, which is used to reinforce the bead cord at clasp ends of a necklace (Fig. 29). It is secured to the necklace with the same method used in attaching jump rings described previously.

The major difference is in the threading of the bouillon onto the bead cord. A short section (¼" to ⅜") is carefully cut from the end of the bouillon. Care must be taken in cutting these pieces as too heavy a

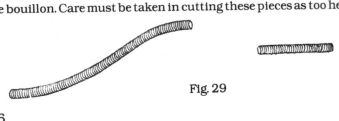

Fig. 29

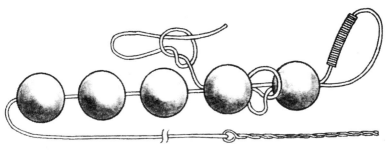

Fig. 30

cutter may crush, flatten or otherwise damage the very fine wire making up the bouillon.

After threading the second and first beads (in that order), insert the cord through the bouillon, carefully, and reinsert the needle into the first bead as shown (Fig. 30). Pull cord to form tight loop of bouillon and repeat procedure on closing ends (Fig. 31), following the steps outlined under jump ring ends, just discussed.

Fig. 31

If the ring on a clasp can be opened, it is attached to the bouillon after completion of the necklace. If the ring cannot be opened, the clasp is attached during the threading of the bouillon.

Crimp Beads

Crimp beads, described in Chapter 4, are used on tigertail and occasionally, heavier monofilament cords. They are not recommended for use with silk or nylon twisted cords, as they have a tendency to cut the cord.

Start by stringing a crimp bead on the end of the tigertail as you would any other bead. Then, string on the clasp or jump ring and bring the cord end back through the crimp bead in the opposite direction, thus forming a loop of cord around the clasp or jump ring. You should have about ½ to ¾ inch free end of cord coming through the crimp bead with the main stringing wire.

Using the tips of chain nose pliers, hold the crimp bead with the hole perpendicular to the jaws of the pliers. Keep both strands of wire

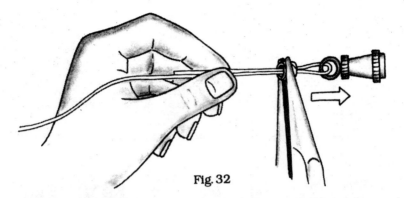

Fig. 32

together and parallel and slide the crimp bead tight against the clasp or jump ring (Fig. 32). Now, squeezing the pliers, flatten the crimp bead using firm pressure, clamping it closed. DO NOT cut off the free end of wire, but proceed by threading on several beads. The first two or three beads should slide over the main stringing wire as well as the

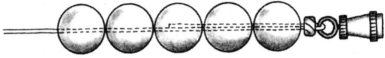

Fig. 33

free end, so as to conceal the short length of starting wire (Fig. 33). This locks the starting end securely and completely hides it for a clean appearance. Continue to thread the remaining beads on the main stringing wire until complete. DO NOT try to knot tigertail — it just can't be done with any assurance that it will stay tied.

Repeat the starting procedure at the finishing end. However, pulling the tigertail tight sometimes is a little difficult. Use this helpful tip to make the job easier — In a small board, hammer a finishing nail or brad into the top about an inch or so from one end, leaving about half of the nail exposed. Be sure that the nail is small enough to go through the hole of the jump ring or clasp you are using on the necklace. String the crimp bead and clasp onto the tigertail and thread the tigertail back through the crimp bead and the last two

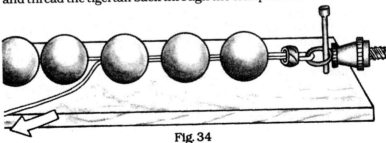

Fig. 34

or three beads on the strand. (This will allow you to keep the finishing end parallel to the main stringing cord when cinching the crimp bead, avoiding any kinks in the end.) Now, slide the jump ring or clasp over the nail in the board (Fig. 34). Anchoring the clasp in this fashion is a tremendous help at this point, as it leaves both hands free to work the slack out of the necklace. While gently pushing the beads toward the clasp, pull the free end of tigertail back toward you until you have taken up all the slack. When the tension is satisfactory, hold the free end of tigertail, maintaining the tension, and with the tips of the chain nose pliers, grip and squeeze the crimp bead tight.

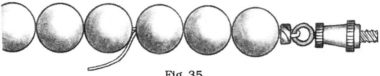

Fig. 35

Cut off the surplus tigertail as close to a bead as possible (Fig. 35). Remember an extra ⅛" of tigertail sticking out between the beads will scratch unbearably and make the necklace unwearable. When properly trimmed, your necklace is complete.

Some fine examples of hand knotted bead necklace designs. Knotting is not limited to any specific type or size of bead.

8. Helpful Tips

1) Outstanding bead stringing is a combination of good workmanship (20%) and design (80%). Good design incorporates the combination of color, shape and size of beads in a creative manner so as to develop interest and beauty to the elements you have before you. Good workmanship is using the proper materials in the correct way. DO take time to be creative. DON'T BE AFRAID to try different combinations of elements and techniques. DO use the proper materials and tools. DON'T try to 'get by' with something you know just isn't right. Practice professionalism every step of the way and you will create a work of art every time.

2) Never force a bead needle through a bead. If it won't go, select a size that will.

3) If a needle should come off the cord in the middle of a project, you can make a "self needle" in silk or nylon twisted cord by applying cement along a 2 to 3 inch length at the end of the cord.

Stretch the cord straight and let dry. Cut the tip of the cord off at an angle and your cord becomes your temporary needle.

4) On cords that tend to stretch, such as twisted nylon or silk, tie a loop in one end and a ½ to ¾ ounce fishing sinker to the other end. Hang the cord by the loop on a picture hook or other spot, high enough so that the sinker is suspended above the floor. Let hang over night to insure your finished necklace is pre-stretched and will stay tight when completed.

5) When disassembling beads, either from a finished necklace or a temporary loose strung strand, work over a 1½ to 2 inch deep tray, pan or box to catch beads as you slide them off.

6) Remember to roll a bead tip closed as outlined in the text. Chain nose pliers may be used, but round nose pliers work even better, rendering a more professional and smoother job.

CORRECT

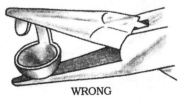

WRONG

7) Use the smallest amount of cement possible to seal knots at the ends of a necklace. You will have greater control by applying cement from the tip of a tooth pick rather than directly from the tube or container. Too much cement may glue several beads together necessitating restringing of the entire necklace.

8) DO NOT try to use super glues (cyanoacrylate) in stringing beads. They are too fluid and move by capillary action, reaching areas you do not want them to.

9) Allow a completed necklace to hang from a hook or nail for 24 hours, if possible, when completed. This permits the beads to "settle" into place and gives a more uniform appearance to the finished work.

9. How To Redrill And Enlarge Bead Holes

A question I often hear is, "How do I enlarge the holes in beads?" Before answering, one must determine why the hole should be enlarged or redrilled. It may simply be to make all the holes a uniform size within a strand of different materials and sizes of beads. Or, it could be to correct a flaw that occurred during the initial drilling operation.

Let's first examine the methods by which beads are originally drilled, and then we can concentrate on solving individual problems in redrilling.

Depending upon the material, size and origin of manufacture, beads are drilled in a variety of ways. The most sophisticated method is by automated, very accurate machines which drill from both sides of the bead with the hole intersecting in the middle. Similarly, hand operated machines may be used, drilling from both sides or only one side. Hand held power drills are also used, usually drilling from both sides, but often from one side, boring the hole completely through the bead in one operation. The last method is by hand reaming, which involves no power tool and is most often reserved for use on seeds, bone, wood or other soft or hollow substances.

When errors occur in any of these drilling methods, different problems are presented to the bead stringer for correction. We will address some of these individual problems later in this chapter.

There are many tools available to aid in correcting drilling errors. High speed steel twist drills can be used on wood, plastic, pearls or metal bead materials. Beads made of glass, crystal, stone and gem materials require the use of diamond drills or reamers.

Drill bits are typically used in a standard drill press, a flexible shaft power grinder or a small hand power grinder. An ordinary hand held electric drill may also be used but, because of their bulkiness and design, they are difficult to control and often lead to broken drill bits, and even worse, splitting, chipping or complete breakage of the bead. The household electric drill should only be used as a last resort and with extreme care.

Metal, wood, and plastic beads may all be safely redrilled while hand held unless too small or excessive heat is noticed by the friction of the drill, in which case, a clamping device of some sort may be necessary. There are several devices on the market for holding beads for drilling. Even a spring-type wooden clothes pin will work in many instances.

Pearls should be handled with very clean hands. It is recommended that clean gloves be worn to avoid body oil and dirt from staining the pearl.

In redrilling procedures, a reciprocating in-and-out motion works best, as opposed to drilling straight through. This allows two very important things to happen: 1) It allows the drill bit to stay cool, and 2) it continually removes debris from the hole and drill bit. Accumulated debris may cause excessive friction producing heat, drill "load-up", and damage to cutting edges.

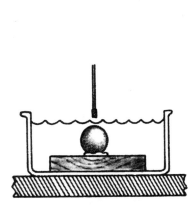

Redrilling glass, crystal, stone and gem beads must be done with either a constant drip or flow of water or with the bead completely submerged in water (see accompanying illustrations). Again, a reciprocal up-and-down or in-and-out action is used to cool as well as clean the drill bit. BE CAREFUL! — You will be working with an electrical appliance around water, a potentially dangerous combination. Make certain that your appliance is properly grounded and well insulated. Do not hold a portable power tool with wet hands. Use care and common sense for safety's sake.

Problems and How to Correct Them

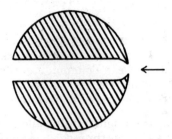

Problem 1

In the original drilling operation, the drill bit did not get all the way through the bead. Approach the hole from the side with the smallest opening, boring only as deep as necessary to clear the unwanted mass. For soft materials a twist drill can be used. On hard materials a diamond reamer will work best.

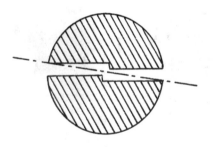

Problem 2

Offset or misaligned holes starting from both sides but failing, or nearly failing, to meet in the center are toughies. For optimum results use a drill press and bore in the path indicated in the illustration, going across the "Z" pattern that was created in the center. This pattern is admittedly difficult to determine in opaque beads, but attempting to redrill in any other direction will only increase the problem. Using small nails or pieces of wire positioned in the holes on both sides of the bead may help in determining the correct path to redrill. Work slowly so the drill will not bend and follow the old hole. It's worth a try, but if you're not successful, don't despair — Even the best of them have to discard an irreparable bead on occasion.

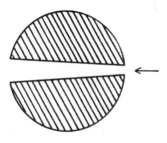

Problem 3

In this problem, the original drill could have "walked" or "wandered" before finding its way through, or the bead could have loosened and turned while being held. To even out the hole, approach the hole from the side with the smallest opening, reaming at least half way through in order to bring about enough uniformity for the bead to ride the cord properly. Since the largest diameter may be oversize, reaming completely to match it may result in a hole that is entirely too large for the bead. Use a twist drill on soft materials, a diamond reamer on ha.d materials.

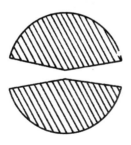

Problem 4

Possibly caused by the same type of occurrence as in problem 3, this bead got it from both sides. Approach from either side with a drill. Since it is tapered, a reamer should not be used here as it may even worsen the problem that already exists.

Problem 5

A misdirected or misaligned hole like this one can be strung as is, but will have a tendency to hang to the side of the necklace as if there were a kink in the cord. Your best chance at salvaging this one, is to

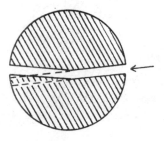

use a drill press and go in one side of the bead slowly boring a straight hole completely through. This will leave you with three holes, but the bead may be usable at the back of the necklace, out of ordinary view. If a large enough bead, a bead cap may conceal the third hole and fit right into the design of your necklace.

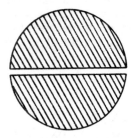

Problem 6

Last, but certainly not least, is the case where the hole is o.k., but it's just too small to accept a proper size cord. Soft materials can be hand held while enlarging the hole with a drill. Hard materials will require that the bead be held in a vice or cemented to a small board and submerged in water as previously shown. Use a drill press for this operation and approach the work very slowly as the drill will have a tendency to wander about the hole already there, ruining the bead, breaking the drill, or at best, creating problem 3 for you to solve.

Some of the tools required for redrilling and repairing beads are shown on the facing page.

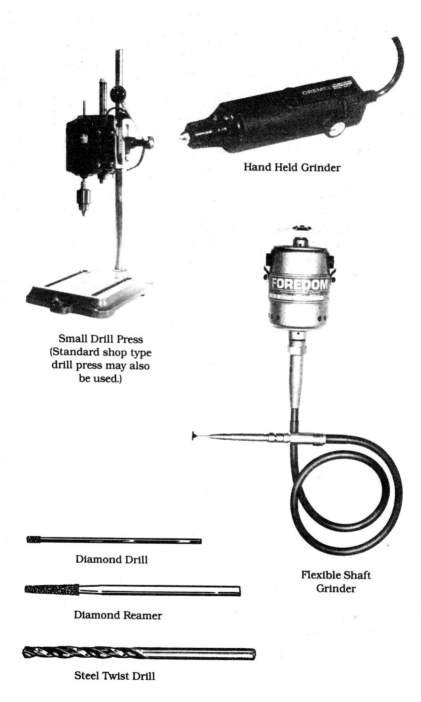

Hand Held Grinder

Small Drill Press
(Standard shop type
drill press may also
be used.)

Flexible Shaft
Grinder

Diamond Drill

Diamond Reamer

Steel Twist Drill

47

NOTES